BIRMINGHAM:
THE FORTIES
REVISITED

Alton & Jo Douglas

A poster on the front of the Municipal Bank, Broad Street, 20th June 1944. Incidentally, the office scenes for the first TV series of "Line of Duty" were filmed inside the building in 2012.

ISBN: 978-1-85858-573-4
Published by Brewin Books Ltd., Doric House, 56 Alcester Road, Studley, Warwickshire B80 7LG.
Printed by Page Brothers.
Layout by Alton and Jo Douglas.

Five Ways, 1948.

Front Cover: Old Square, looking down on Corporation Street from Lewis's, 1940.

CONTENTS

BREWIN BOOKS LTD

Doric House, 56 Alcester Road,
Studley, Warwickshire B80 7LG
Tel: 01527 854228 Fax: 01527 852746
VAT Registration No. 705 0077 73

Dear Nostalgic,

Alright, why the forties again? Well, it was certainly the most dangerous period in the city's history, the most challenging but also, for some, the most exciting days of their lives. It was a decade made up of two halves - conflict and recovery - the war years showed us at our resilient best and the second half confirmed the idea that we could gather ourselves together and move on. However, humour was never far from the surface either and I can remember seeing, chalked on the side of the police station, the irresistible, "STAY GOOD - WE'RE STILL OPEN!" We thought, therefore, it would be revealing to show, as well as the dramatic images, the important part that entertainment played during those difficult years. Interestingly, by the way, the Birmingham Hippodrome was always known as "The Hippodrome" (or "The Hipp") whereas the Aston Hippodrome was always referred to by its full name.

Once again, many thanks to all our friends (some now sadly departed) who gave us access to treasured and carefully preserved photographs, magazines, newspapers, wartime leaflets, posters and postcards. Also, I have to reveal that we have been constantly collecting material since our first book, "Birmingham at War Volume 1", was published thirty five years ago!

So, lets start in the fifth month of the war and marvel at ten years of courage and awe-inspiring determination.

Yours, in friendship,

High Street, from Martineau Street, 1949.

Lodge Road/All Saints Road, Aston, 28th January 1940.

ZIPP IT

CARELESS TALK COSTS LIVES

Customers being shown how the rationing coupon system works, January 1940.

A pack of patriotic playing cards - Winston Churchill was the First Lord of the Admiralty until he became Prime Minister on the 10th May 1940.

Delivering Anderson air raid shelters, Somerville Road, Small Heath, 1940. One and a half million shelters were distributed before the outbreak of war. Householders were charged £7, those earning less than £5 a week received them free. Despite several false alarms they were not in regular use until August.

IF YOU ARE BOMBED OUT
and have no friends to go to

ask a
POLICEMAN
or your **WARDEN**
where to find your
REST CENTRE

in a raid

Open your door to passers-by — They need shelter too

AIR RAID
ALERT
HAS SOUNDED

AIR RAID SHELTER

PERSONS MAY SHELTER HERE AT THEIR OWN RISK AFTER THE TAKE COVER NOTICE HAS BEEN GIVEN

Persons sheltering are not allowed to take Birds, Dogs, Cats and other Animals, as well as Mailcarts, on to the Company's premises.

RATS

are waiting to share our Air Raid Shelters.

IF

you do not favour **A.R.P. FOR RATS** keep all shelters clean and tidy. Leave no scraps of food about.

Dudley Road Hospital staff and air raid patrols, 1940.

Dismantling the Cathedral railings for salvage,
Colmore Row, 1940.

FRY'S COCOA

Rich in nerve food!

Kings Norton Park, c 1940.

The Birmingham Hospital Centre, Edgbaston, 1940. It later became the Queen Elizabeth Hospital.

Moseley Village, 1940. The post office is on the left.

Opposition joins the Government

10 May, 1940

SIR ARCHIBALD SINCLAIR

THE RT. HON. WINSTON S. CHURCHILL

Previously Mr. Churchill had held Cabinet office as First Lord of the Admiralty; Mr. Attlee and Sir Archibald Sinclair were Leaders of the two Parliamentary Oppositions, Labour and Liberal respectively; Mr. Greenwood, Secretary of the Labour Party Research Department; Mr. Alexander, Leader of the Parliamentary Co-operative Party; Mr. Morrison, Leader of the London County Council; Mr. Bevin, member of the Executive of the Trades Union Congress, and Mr. Dalton, a member of the Labour Party's National Executive.

MR. ERNEST BEVIN

MR. HERBERT MORRISON

MR. A. V. ALEXANDER

MR. C. R. ATTLEE

MR. ARTHUR GREENWOOD

MR. HUGH DALTON

RESIGNATION OF MR. CHAMBERLAIN. Confidence in the Government led by Mr. Chamberlain was seriously undermined by the general conduct of the war, and after a debate on the question in the Commons on 8 May, Mr. Chamberlain invited the Opposition to serve under him in a reconstructed Cabinet. Labour, however, refused and on 10 May the Premier resigned and was succeeded by Mr. Winston Churchill. Above is seen the new Premier together with some of the new Ministers. The new War Cabinet consisted of the Premier, who also became Minister of Defence; Mr. Chamberlain, Lord President of the Council; Lord Halifax, Foreign Secretary; Mr. C. R. Attlee, Lord Privy Seal, and Mr. Arthur Greenwood, Minister without Portfolio. Other Ministers were: Mr. A. V. Alexander, Admiralty; Mr. Anthony Eden, War; Sir Archibald Sinclair, Air; Sir John Simon, Lord Chancellor; Sir Kingsley Wood, Exchequer; Sir John Anderson, Home Secretary; Lord Lloyd, Colonies; Sir Andrew Duncan, Board of Trade; Mr. Herbert Morrison, Supply; Mr. Duff Cooper, Information; Mr. Ernest Bevin, Labour and National Service; Mr. L. S. Amery, India and Burma; Mr. Malcolm MacDonald, Health; Lord Woolton, Food; Viscount Caldicote, Dominions; Mr. Ernest Brown, Scotland; Lord Beaverbrook, Aircraft Production; Mr. H. Ramsbotham, Education; Mr. Robert Hudson, Agriculture; Sir John Reith, Transport; Mr. Ronald Cross, Shipping, and Mr. Hugh Dalton, Economic Warfare.

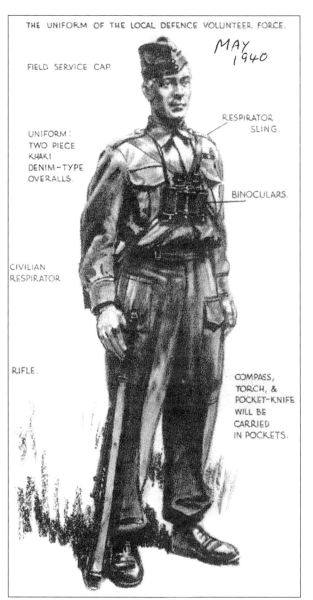

THE UNIFORM OF THE LOCAL DEFENCE VOLUNTEER FORCE.

MAY 1940

FIELD SERVICE CAP.

RESPIRATOR SLING.

UNIFORM: TWO PIECE KHAKI DENIM-TYPE OVERALLS.

BINOCULARS.

CIVILIAN RESPIRATOR.

RIFLE.

COMPASS, TORCH, & POCKET-KNIFE WILL BE CARRIED IN POCKETS.

The Local Defence Volunteers became known as the Home Guard in July 1940. Winston Churchill thought that the original name was demeaning.

WOMEN OF BRITAIN
COME INTO THE FACTORIES

ASK AT ANY EMPLOYMENT EXCHANGE FOR ADVICE AND FULL DETAILS

Copy Number: 2.

S E C R E T.

August 1940

AUXILIARY UNITS, HOME FORCES

A. Organization etc.

Object:

1. The object of Auxiliary Units, Home Forces, on the fighting side, is to build up, within the general body of the Home Guards, a series of small local units whose role is to act offensively on the flanks and in the rear of any German troops who may obtain a temporary foothold in this country.

The other role is Intelligence.

Method of Employment:

2. These Auxiliary Units are equipped with special Molotov bombs, delay action fuzes and plastic H.E., incendiary bombs and devices of various kinds from non-military stocks, as well as the rifle and grenade. Their task is to harry and embarrass the enemy by all means in their power from the first day he lands, their particular targets being tanks and lorries in lager, ammunition dumps, H.Q.s, small straggling parties and posts etc. Their object is, in co-operation with the regular forces, to prevent the invader establishing a secure foothold, and thus to facilitate his defeat.

3. These units must operate mainly by night and therefore are constituted entirely from local men who know their countryside intimately, i.e. farmers, game-keepers, hunt servants etc. under a selected local leader. In certain areas where woodlands or heath are of considerable extent, particular units have the special role of occupying prepared 'hide-outs' as a base for operations. These hide-outs are being prepared.

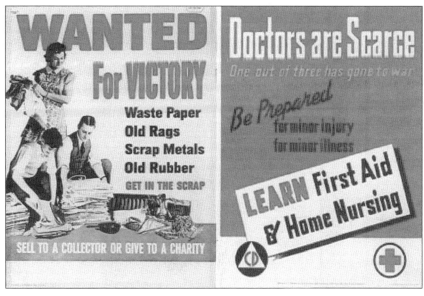

WANTED For VICTORY
Waste Paper
Old Rags
Scrap Metals
Old Rubber
GET IN THE SCRAP
SELL TO A COLLECTOR OR GIVE TO A CHARITY

Doctors are Scarce
One out of three has gone to war
Be Prepared for minor injury for minor illness
LEARN First Aid & Home Nursing

Congreve Street/Edmund Street, c 1940.

Stratford Road, Sparkbrook, 1940.

Families discuss the destruction of their Anderson shelters, Oldknow Road, Small Heath, August 1940.

Taxis powered by gas, Suffolk Street, 1940. The supply would last for up to 20 miles.

Searchlights illuminate the sky allowing the anti-aircraft guns or fighter pilots to engage the enemy aircraft, 1940.

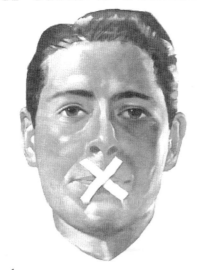

Pipe Hayes Home Guard Parade and March Past outside the Apollo Cinema, Tyburn Road, August 1940.

At the end of their shift workers undergo Home Guard training, Wolseley Motors, Drews Lane, Ward End, 1940.

Digging for Victory, Anstey College, Chester Road, Erdington.

Issued by the Ministry of Information on behalf of the War Office and the Ministry of Home Security

STAY WHERE YOU ARE

IF this island is invaded by sea or air everyone who is not under orders must stay where he or she is. This is not simply advice : it is an order from the Government, and you must obey it just as soldiers obey their orders. Your order is "Stay Put", but remember that this does not apply until invasion comes.

Why must I stay put ?

Because in France, Holland and Belgium, the Germans were helped by the people who took flight before them. Great crowds of refugees blocked all roads. The soldiers who could have defended them could not get at the enemy. The enemy used the refugees as a human shield. These refugees were got out on to the roads by rumour and false orders. Do not be caught out in this way. Do not take any notice of any story telling what the enemy has done or where he is. Do not take orders except from the Military, the Police, the Home Guard (L.D.V.) and the A.R.P. authorities or wardens.

What will happen to me if I don't stay put ?

If you do not stay put you will stand a very good chance of being killed. The enemy may machine-gun you from the air in order to increase panic, or you may run into enemy forces which have landed behind you. An official German message was captured in Belgium which ran :

"Watch for civilian refugees on the roads. Harass them as much as possible."

Our soldiers will be hurrying to drive back the invader and will not be able to stop and help you.

Planes lost in fighting over Britain and the coast, 8—19 August, 1940 (R.A.F. official figures)			
	German planes lost	British planes lost	British pilots safe
August 8	61	13	3
„ 9	1	—	—
„ 10	1	1	—
„ 11	65	26	2
„ 12	62	13	1
„ 13	78	13	10
„ 14	31	7	2
„ 15	180	34	17
„ 16	75	22	14
„ 17	1	—	—
„ 18	152	22	8
„ 19	4	—	—
TOTAL	711	156	57

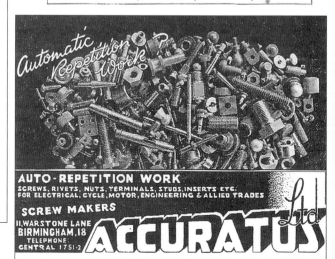

The Prime Minister's wife, Mrs Churchill, talks to Birmingham rescue crews, 16th October 1940.

Stratton & Co. Ltd. (mnfr. jewellers and wireless receiving sets) Bromsgrove Street, October 1940.

A captured German Messerschmitt stands in front of the Birmingham Municipal Bank, Broad Street, 1940.

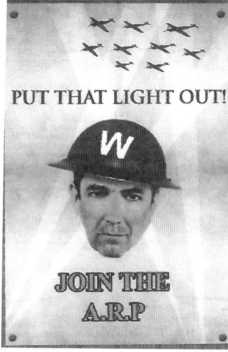

PUBLIC NOTICE

BIRMINGHAM MEALS SERVICE

A CENTRE AT WHICH HOT MEALS
CAN BE BOUGHT CHEAPLY FOR
CONSUMPTION OFF THE PREMISES
WILL BE OPENED ON
WEDNESDAY, 11th DECEMBER, 1940,
AT
SUMMER LANE COUNCIL SCHOOL.

FACTORY WORKERS AND RESIDENTS
IN THE AREA ARE INVITED TO
CALL, BUY AND TRY.

PLEASE BRING YOUR OWN DISHES, JUGS OR BASINS
P. D. INNES,
Chief Education Officer.

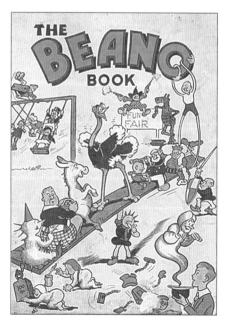

A mobile post office in a bombed area, 1941.

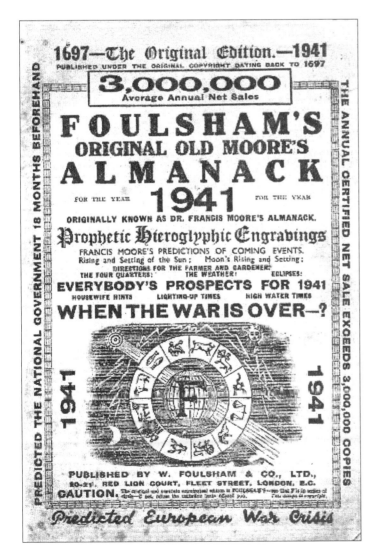

CITY OF BIRMINGHAM
AIR RAID PRECAUTIONS

This is to certify that

_____

is a member of a voluntary fire-fighting party which is recognised by the Birmingham City Council, and possesses the power of entry and of taking steps for extinguishing fire or for protecting property or rescuing persons or property from fire, which are conferred by the Fire Precautions (Access to Premises) Order, 1940.

F. H. C. WILTSHIRE,
Town Clerk and A.R.P. Controller.

Date of appointment ....

Signature of Holder ....

F24888-B1 (k)

BSA (Birmingham Small Arms) Tool Room staff, Armoury Road, Small Heath, 1941.

BSA Administrative staff, 1941.

Prince of Wales Theatre, suffered a direct hit and was completely destroyed, Broad Street, 10th April 1941.

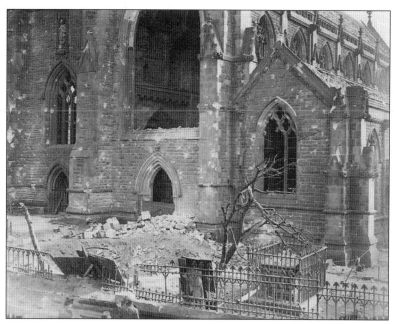

St Martin's damaged by bombs, Bull Ring, 10th April 1941.

St Martin's, Bull Ring, 10th April 1941.

The morning after, Bull Ring, 10th April 1941.

Finding it difficult to get to work, in the city, 10th April 1941.

Food Guide for Children of All Ages

APPROXIMATE QUANTITIES PER DAY

	Food.	9 months to 1 year.	1—2.	2—6.	6—12.	12—18.
	Milk	1–1½ pint	1 pint	1 pint	½-pt. + school milk	½-pt. + school milk, or ½-pt. after leaving school
Per day	Potatoes	1 tablespoon	1 tablespoon	1–2 heaped tablespoons	2–5 heaped tablespoons	5–8 heaped tablespoons
per day	National bread	1 slice	½–1 slice	1½–4 slices	4–7 slices	7–14 slices
per day	Salad or raw vegetable	Orange juice or b'kcurrant puree or rose hip syrup	Fruit juice or 1½-oz. raw vegetable after 18 months	½–1 oz.	1–2 oz.	2–3 oz.
Per day	Green vegetable	1 tablespoon	1 tablespoon	1–2 heaped tablespoons	2–3 heaped tablespoons	2–3 heaped tablespoons
		or	or	or	and or	and
	Root vegetable	1 tablespoon	1 tablespoon	1–2 heaped tablespoons	2–3 heaped tablespoons	2–3 heaped tablespoons
per day	Margarine & Butter	½-oz.	¼–½ oz.	½–¾ oz.	Full ration	Full ration
per week	Egg (if available)	2 per week	2–3 per week	4 per week	1 per week	1 per week
per week	Cheese	—	1–1½ oz.	1½–3 oz.	3 oz. (or full ration)	3 oz. (or full ration)
per week	Meat	Liver (only) 1 tablespoon	3 tablespoons (1 liver)	3–5 tablespns.	5–10 tablespns (or full ration)	1 lb. raw wt. (or full ration)
per week	Fish (if available)	2 tablespoons (fresh)	3 tablespoons (fresh)	3–4 tablespns (fresh or salt)	4–9 tablespns (fresh or salt)	1 lb. raw wt. (fresh or salt)
per week	Bacon	1–1½ oz. bacon fat	1–2 oz.	2–4 oz.	4 oz. (or full ration)	4 oz. (or full ration)

"Mom said to keep our gas mask on if we go out." c 1941.

Air Raid Precaution (ARP) Wardens, 1941.

ARP Officers' kitchen, Sparkhill, c 1941.

Birmingham members of F26, C Coy, 41st Battalion,
Home Guard, 1941.

The 43rd Warwickshire Battalion Home Guard,
Longbridge, 1941. It was almost completely made up of
Austin employees.

The Prime Minister, Winston Churchill, visits the Wolseley Works,
Drews Lane, Ward End, 13th September 1941.

Women workers from W. Canning & Co. Ltd. (mnfrs of electro-plating and
polishers plant and material) Great Hampton Street, 1941.

CARELESS TALK
MAY COST HIS LIFE

DON'T TALK ABOUT AERODROMES or AIRCRAFT FACTORIES

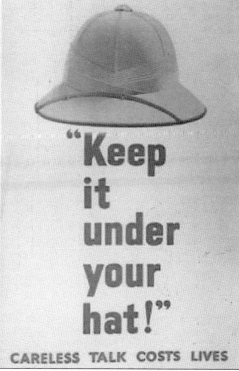

"Keep
it
under
your
hat!"

CARELESS TALK COSTS LIVES

INDOOR SHELTER beds are 6 ft. 6 in. long and 4 ft. wide and weigh 5 cwt., about the weight of a grand piano. The shelters will be supplied in parts and must be put together by the householder. Their adoption by the Ministry of Home Security followed upon the discovery that houses form a better protection against bomb than it was originally supposed they would do.

Photo, courtesy of the Ministry of Information

The Morrison shelter, free to households with incomes of less than £350 p.a., otherwise it costs £8, November 1941.

The Town Hall protected from bomb blast by sandbags, 1941.

Birmingham evacuees in Gotham, in Nottinghamshire, 1941.

RATIONING OF CLOTHING: NUMBER OF COUPONS NEEDED

Mr. Oliver Lyttelton, President of the Board of Trade announced his scheme for the immediate rationing of clothing, including footwear. Each person will have 66 clothing coupons to last for twelve months

MEN and BOYS	Adult	Child	WOMEN and GIRLS	Adult	Child
Unlined mackintosh or cape	9	7	Lined mackintoshes, or coats (over 28 in. long)	14	11
Other mackintoshes, or raincoat, or overcoat	16	11	Jacket, or short coat (under 28 in. long)	11	8
Coat, or jacket, or blazer or like garment	13	8	Dress, or gown, or frock—woollen	11	8
Waistcoat, or pull-over, or cardigan, or jersey	5	3	Dress, or gown, or frock—other material	7	5
Trousers (other than fustian or corduroy)	8	6	Gym tunic, or girl's skirt with bodice	8	6
Fustian or corduroy trousers	5	5	Blouse, or sports shirt, or cardigan, or jumper	5	3
Shorts	5	3	Skirt, or divided skirt	7	5
Overalls, or dungarees or like garment	6	4	Overalls, or dungarees or like garment	6	4
Dressing-gown or bathing-gown	8	6	Apron, or pinafore	3	2
Nightshirt or pair of pyjamas	8	6	Pyjamas	8	6
Shirt, or combinations—woollen	8	6	Nightdress	6	5
Shirt, or combinations—other material	5	4	Petticoat, or slip, or combination, or cami-knickers	4	3
Pants, or vest, or bathing costume, or child's blouse	4	2	Other undergarments, including corsets	3	2
Pair of socks or stockings	3	1	Pair of stockings	2	1
Collar, or tie, or pair of cuffs	1	1	Pair of socks (ankle length)	1	1
Two handkerchiefs	1	1	Collar, or tie, or pair of cuffs	1	1
Scarf, or pair of gloves or mittens	2	2	Two handkerchiefs	1	1
Pair of slippers or goloshes	4	2	Scarf, or pair of gloves or mittens, or muff	2	2
Pair of boots or shoes	7	3	Pair of slippers, boots or shoes	5	3
Pair of leggings, gaiters or spats	3	2			
CLOTH. Coupons needed per yard depend on the width.			KNITTING WOOL. 1 coupon for two ounces.		

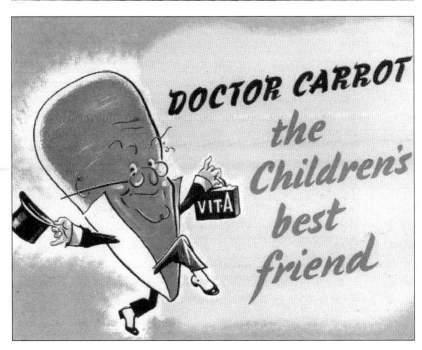

DOCTOR CARROT the Children's best friend

THE ATTACK ON THE ARMS TOWNS

Dates of main raids	Estimated enemy planes engaged	Total civilians killed in all raids to end of 1941
COVENTRY		
14th November	400	
8th April	300	1,236
10th April	200	
BIRMINGHAM		
1st November	—	
19th November	350	
22nd November	200	
3rd December	50	2,162
11th December	200	
9th and 10th April	250	

A barrage balloon used to deter low-flying German aircraft, 1942. Alton: "I can remember, when I was about 4, crying when I saw one deflated on its side in Digby Park. I thought someone had killed it!"

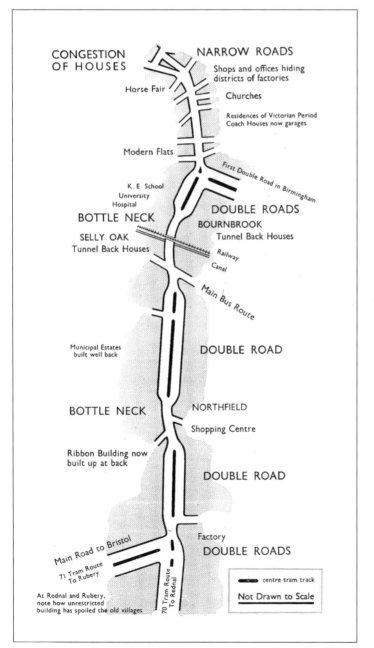

CONGESTION OF HOUSES

NARROW ROADS
Shops and offices hiding districts of factories

Horse Fair

Churches

Residences of Victorian Period Coach Houses now garages

Modern Flats

First Double Road in Birmingham

K. E School
University
Hospital

DOUBLE ROADS

BOTTLE NECK

BOURNBROOK
Tunnel Back Houses

SELLY OAK
Tunnel Back Houses

Railway

Canal

Main Bus Route

Municipal Estates
built well back

DOUBLE ROAD

BOTTLE NECK

NORTHFIELD

Shopping Centre

Ribbon Building now
built up at back

DOUBLE ROAD

Main Road to Bristol

Factory

DOUBLE ROADS

71 Tram Route
To Rubery

70 Tram Route
To Rednal

At Rednal and Rubery,
note how unrestricted
building has spoiled the old villages

centre tram track

Not Drawn to Scale

Singer, Anne Shelton, makes her first appearance at the Hippodrome, 19th January 1942. She was accompanied by the brilliant, blind pianist, George Shearing.

Vic Oliver, Austrian-born comedian, actor and musician, was Roy Plomley's first guest on the long-running BBC radio programme, "Desert Island Discs", 29th January 1942. He was a regular at the Hippodrome and the Town Hall over the years.

The Home Guard prepare road blocks, 1942.

Troops practising wall climbing at a street fighting school in the city, 1942.

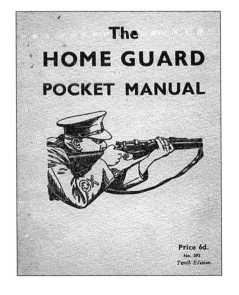

25

Queen Mary visits the BSA, 1942.

BSA Folding Motor Cycle, 1942. They were made for the
British Airborne Offensive.

High Street, looking towards Dale End, with Carrs Lane first on the right, 1942.

The Bull Ring, 1942.

An unexploded bomb that landed on RG Boardman & Co. (engineers/small tools) Summer Row, 1942.

Control Room, Fire Service Headquarters, Corporation Street/Aston Street, c 1942.

The "Shadow Factory Tunnels" at the Austin where hundreds of women workers helped the war effort, Longbridge, c 1942.

Pearks grocery store, Coventry Road (opposite Kings Road) Hay Mills, 1942.

Practice by members of the Women's Fire Guard, Boxfoldia Ltd., Dale Road, Bournbrook 1942.

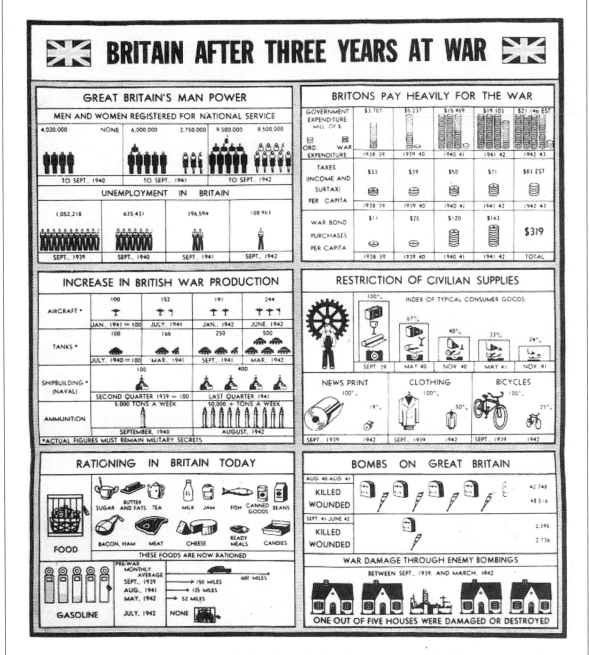

BRITAIN AFTER THREE YEARS AT WAR

This pictorial chart gives just a slight idea of the three years of fighting and sacrifice which the people of Britain have dedicated towards smashing the Axis.

It would be impossible to show every restriction that Britain has submitted to gladly and willingly during these first three years of war. To show how even the limited supplies of food available are not always obtainable by the public, how unrationed foods are frequently so scarce that few people can obtain them at all, how furniture and household linen, pots and pans are practically unobtainable.

But as civilian supplies of food, clothing and fuel grow smaller, Britain's war effort grows larger. Savings campaigns exist in every village, the sale of certificates and war bonds is ever on the increase, interest-free loans are made to the government.

Every factory is working at top speed, twenty-four hours a day turning out an ever-increasing number of tanks, aircraft and munitions with which to deal the death blow to Hitler and his Axis partners.

The British can laugh at shortages and rationing because they know that by doing so they are contributing to victory.

(F 1695) Wt 530M 4A6 3 43 Co 957 FOSH & CROSS LTD.

Richard Tauber, the world-famous Austrian tenor, appears in "Old Chelsea", Theatre Royal, November 1942. The following year he was back, at the same theatre, in the same musical!

DECEMBER 1942

RAF Wythall was responsible for the Barrage Balloon defence of the southern parts of Birmingham, 1943.

For Economy's
Sake drink

"Ty·phoo" TEA

Ask your
grocer for it !

Should you have
any difficulty in
obtaining your
supplies, write to us

TY-PHOO TEA LTD., BORDESLEY STREET, BIRMINGHAM 5.

Number 6 Barrage Balloon Centre, RAF Wythall.

BILE BEANS

For Radiant
HEALTH
and a Lovely
FIGURE

A mobile support unit at the First Aid Post,
Grove Lane Baths, Handsworth, 1943.

CLEAN HANDS
GUARDIANS OF HEALTH

ALWAYS
WASH HANDS THOROUGHLY — CLEAN FINGER NAILS
1. BEFORE BEGINNING TO PREPARE OR SERVE FOOD
2. ALWAYS AFTER USING THE TOILET
3. WHENEVER HANDS BECOME SOILED
GET THE CLEAN HANDS HABIT

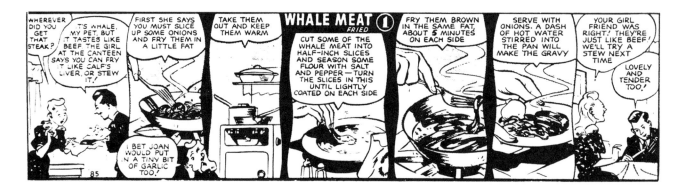

Ivy Benson who, with her All Girl Orchestra, became the leader of one of the BBC's resident dance bands in 1943.

Phil Tuffey and his Blue Rhythm Orchestra with vocalist, Thelma White, Hippodrome, 16th April 1943. It was a concert in aid of the RAF Benevolent Fund.

Stirchley Baths, c 1943. Dancing to Den Jones and his Orchestra.

33

IN BIRMINGHAM

OVER 100,000 PEOPLE (or more than one out of ten) still live in back-to-back houses.

OVER 330,000 PEOPLE (or more than one out of three) live in houses of this type.

OVER 350,000 PEOPLE (or more than one out of three) live in houses built since the last war.

Typical slum-like workshops still to be found in the Jewellery Quarter in 1943.

WHEN WE BUILD AGAIN WE MUST

No more playgrounds like this

No more congested streets

No more overcrowded schools

NOT REPEAT OUR OLD MISTAKES—

No more dingy courts

No more drab districts

No more huddled houses

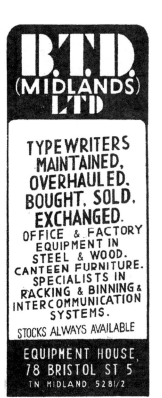

A huge banner displayed on the side of the Town Hall, 1943.

Wings for Victory Week, 26th June 1943.

Women's Land Army volunteers set out to work, 1943.

They heeded the call!

COMRADES IN ARMS!

BRITAIN AND THE U.S.S.R.

ЖЕЛАЕМ УСПЕХА И СКОРОЙ ПОБЕДЫ
НАШИМ РУССКИМ ТОВАРИЩАМ

Electric cargo cars built by Birmingham women for the Russians, 1943.
They would have been battery powered. The exact location would not have
been disclosed for reasons of security.

GERMANY STRICTLY OBSERVING GENEVA CONVENTION

For every soldier, even the bravest, the moment may
arrive when fighting on would mean senseless self-
destruction and no benefit to his country. It is
recognized by all nations at war that under such cir-
cumstances the soldiers are justified in surrendering.
If you should face a like situation, keep the following points well in mind:

FIRST:

You will be taken for a few days to a Dulag
(transit camp) right behind the front. The Dulags
are no hotels. They are fitted out simply as the near-
ness of the front demands, but you will be safe and
well-treated. You may send home a message at once
via radio "Jerry's Front Calling" telling your wife
and family you are alive. If you are wounded or sick,
you will immediately receive the best of medical care
exactly like a German soldier.

SECOND:

You will be transferred to a Stalag (permanent camp).
The Stalags are up-to-date camps with all convenien-
ces. The food is prepared in modern kitchens.

German propaganda leaflet.

HELP BRITAIN FINISH THE JOB!

Wilbert Awdry, author of the "Thomas The Tank" books, wrote his first story, "The Three Railway Engines", in 1943. He was the curate at St Nicholas Church, in Kings Norton, at the time.

Members of the Alexandra Theatre's Repertory Company, Vanda Godsell and David Ashe in "Quiet Wedding", 1943.

The Ritz cinema, Bordesley Green East, 1943. The film was "The Man In Grey", starring James Mason and Margaret Lockwood.

Books on the History of Birmingham

The following list is a selection of some of the many books dealing with Birmingham. Nearly all are available at Branches of the Birmingham Public Libraries, as well as the Central Library. The staff, at the Central Reference Library especially, will be pleased to give information and assistance.

ALLEN (G. C.). *The Industrial Development of Birmingham and of the Black Country, 1860-1927. Illus. & Maps.* 1929.

AUDEN (G. A.) ed. *A handbook for Birmingham and the neighbourhood, prepared for the 83rd meeting of the British Association for the Advancement of Science.* 1913.

BUNCE (J. T.), VINCE (C. A.) and JONES (J. T.). *History of the Corporation of Birmingham. With a sketch of the earlier government.* 5 vols. 1878-1940.

COURT (W. H. B.). *The Rise of the Midland industries, 1600-1838.* 1938.

DENT (R. K.). *The Making of Birmingham: the rise and growth of the Midland metropolis. Illus.* 1894.

DICKINSON (H. W.). *Matthew Boulton. Ports. & Illus.* 1937.

DICKINSON (H. W.) and JENKINS (R.). *James Watt and the Steam Engine. Memorial volume prepared for the Committee of the Watt Centenary Commemoration, Birmingham, 1919. Ports., Illus. & Maps.* 1927.

GILL (C.). *Studies in Midland history (includes Birmingham in the 16th century and the Manor of Handsworth). Illus. & Maps.* 1930.

HILL (J.). *The Book-makers of old Birmingham: authors, printers and booksellers. Illus.* 1907.

HUTTON (W.). *History of Birmingham to the end of 1780. Map & Illus.* 1781. Note.—*There are many editions of this work.*

LANGFORD (J. A.). *A Century of Birmingham life: a chronicle of local events, 1741 to 1841. 2nd edn. 2 vols.* 1870-71.

LANGFORD (J. A.). *Modern Birmingham and its institutions: a chronicle of local events, 1841 to 1871. 2 vols.* 1873-77.

MUIRHEAD (J. H.) ed. *Birmingham institutions. Ports. & Illus.* 1911.

MUIRHEAD (J. H.) ed. *Nine famous Birmingham men (J. Priestley, George Dixon, George Dawson, James Watt, John Bright, Bishop Westcott, Cardinal Newman, Sir E. Burne-Jones, R. W. Dale). Ports.* 1909.

SMITH (J. T.). *Memorials of old Birmingham. Men and names: 13th to 16th centuries. With particulars as to the earliest church of the Reformation (i.e. St. John's, Deritend). Illus.* 1864.

"IT ALL DEPENDS ON ME"

To :—

Work as never before

Lend for all I'm worth

Dig for Victory

Manage cheerfully with my rations

Avoid all waste

Knit for the Forces

Give my best to voluntary war work

—⋅—

In Germany — it all depends on Hitler

Here we can all accept the challenge and say—

"IT ALL DEPENDS ON ME"

CALENDAR for 1944

JANUARY		FEBRUARY		MARCH	
S	- 2 9 16 23 30	S	... 6 13 20 27	S	... 5 12 19 26
M	- 3 10 17 24 31	M	... 7 14 21 28	M	- 6 13 20 27
Tu	- 4 11 18 25 ...	Tu	1 8 15 22 29	Tu	- 7 14 21 28
W	- 5 12 19 26 ...	W	2 9 16 23 ...	W	1 8 15 22 29
Th	- 6 13 20 27 ...	Th	3 10 17 24 ...	Th	2 9 16 23 30
F	- 7 14 21 28 ...	F	4 11 18 25 ...	F	3 10 17 24 31
S	1 8 15 22 29 ...	S	5 12 19 26 ...	S	4 11 18 25 ...

APRIL		MAY		JUNE	
S	- 2 9 16 23 30	S	... 7 14 21 28	S	- 4 11 18 25
M	- 3 10 17 24 ...	M	1 8 15 22 29	M	... 5 12 19 26
Tu	- 4 11 18 25 ...	Tu	2 9 16 23 30	Tu	... 6 13 20 27
W	- 5 12 19 26 ...	W	3 10 17 24 31	W	... 7 14 21 28
Th	- 6 13 20 27 ...	Th	4 11 18 25 ...	Th	1 8 15 22 29
F	- 7 14 21 28 ...	F	5 12 19 26 ...	F	2 9 16 23 30
S	1 8 15 22 29 ...	S	6 13 20 27 ...	S	3 10 17 24 ...

JULY		AUGUST		SEPTEMBER	
S	- 2 9 16 23 30	S	... 6 13 20 27	S	... 3 10 17 24
M	- 3 10 17 24 31	M	... 7 14 21 28	M	... 4 11 18 25
Tu	- 4 11 18 25 ...	Tu	1 8 15 22 29	Tu	... 5 12 19 26
W	- 5 12 19 26 ...	W	2 9 16 23 30	W	... 6 13 20 27
Th	- 6 13 20 27 ...	Th	3 10 17 24 31	Th	... 7 14 21 28
F	- 7 14 21 28 ...	F	4 11 18 25 ...	F	1 8 15 22 29
S	1 8 15 22 29 ...	S	5 12 19 26 ...	S	2 9 16 23 30

OCTOBER		NOVEMBER		DECEMBER	
S	1 8 15 22 29	S	... 5 12 19 26	S	- 3 10 17 24 31
M	2 9 16 23 30	M	... 6 13 20 27	M	- 4 11 18 25 ...
Tu	3 10 17 24 31	Tu	... 7 14 21 28	Tu	- 5 12 19 26 ...
W	4 11 18 25 ...	W	1 8 15 22 29	W	- 6 13 20 27 ...
Th	5 12 19 26 ...	Th	2 9 16 23 30	Th	- 7 14 21 28 ...
F	6 13 20 27 ...	F	3 10 17 24 ...	F	1 8 15 22 29 ...
S	7 14 21 28 ...	S	4 11 18 25 ...	S	2 9 16 23 30 ...

Good Friday - APRIL 7   Whit-Monday - MAY 29.
Easter Monday - APRIL 10.   Aug. Bank Holiday - AUG. 7.

FOR VICTORY AND FREEDOM

"IT ALL DEPENDS ON ME"

Gas Street Basin, c 1944.

St Martin's Flats, Dymoke Street, Highgate.

SAVE WASTE AND START A PIG CLUB

FACTORIES, SCHOOLS, POLICE POSTS, A.R.P. STATIONS— ANY ORGANISED BODY OF INDIVIDUALS CAN HELP THE WAR EFFORT, AND THEMSELVES, BY STARTING A CO-OPERATIVE PIG CLUB

JOSEPH LUCAS LTD.
Head Offices & Works
GT. KING STREET · BIRMINGHAM

SUPREME HEADQUARTERS
ALLIED EXPEDITIONARY FORCE

Soldiers, Sailors and Airmen of the Allied Expeditionary Force!

You are about to embark upon the Great Crusade, toward which we have striven these many months. The eyes of the world are upon you. The hopes and prayers of liberty-loving people everywhere march with you. In company with our brave Allies and brothers-in-arms on other Fronts, you will bring about the destruction of the German war machine, the elimination of Nazi tyranny over the oppressed peoples of Europe, and security for ourselves in a free world.

Your task will not be an easy one. Your enemy is well trained, well equipped and battle-hardened. He will fight savagely.

But this is the year 1944! Much has happened since the Nazi triumphs of 1940-41. The United Nations have inflicted upon the Germans great defeats, in open battle, man-to-man. Our air offensive has seriously reduced their strength in the air and their capacity to wage war on the ground. Our Home Fronts have given us an overwhelming superiority in weapons and munitions of war, and placed at our disposal great reserves of trained fighting men. The tide has turned! The free men of the world are marching together to Victory!

I have full confidence in your courage, devotion to duty and skill in battle. We will accept nothing less than full Victory!

Good Luck! And let us all beseech the blessing of Almighty God upon this great and noble undertaking.

Dwight Eisenhower

6.6.44

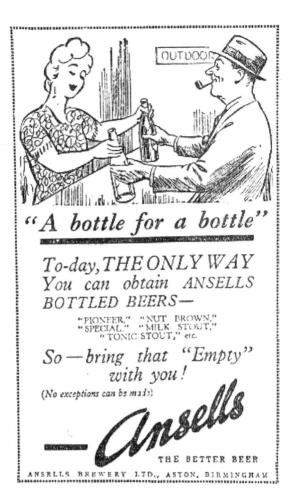

Mrs Frost washes the clothes using a dolly tub, Woodbine Villa, Hay Mills, 1944. Her daughter, Lillian, won second prize (10 shillings) in Redhill Road Schools' photographic competition with this picture. It's amazing that, with the shortage of film during the war years, they were able to hold such a competition!

Vera Lynn, "The Forces Sweetheart", in another of her many wartime broadcasts, 1944.

A Cromwell tank involved in the Normandy landings, 1944.
They were manufactured at the Birmingham Railway
Carriage and Wagon Company.

HMS Birmingham, 1944.

"SALUTE THE SOLDIER WEEK"
Broad Street, 20th June 1944.

Radio Times (incorporating World-Radio)   July 14 1944
Vol 84 No. 1085 Registered at the G.P.O as a Newspaper

RADIO TIMES
JOURNAL OF THE BRITISH BROADCASTING CORPORATION

GLENN MILLER

Programme

Sgt. JOHNNY DESMOND used to sing with Gene Krupa

GLENN MILLER, the Moonlight Serenader

DANCE-music enthusiasts in the A.E.F. will have noticed a lot of new names in their programmes since last Sunday, and among them one that is known wherever swing has a following. Glenn Miller, the Moonlight Serenader, is now broadcasting regularly in the A.E.F. Programme.

Glenn Miller has not got a ' name band ' nowadays. He is a captain in the U.S. Army, and for two years he has been running a band for the Air Forces Training Command. Now he has brought his band to Britain and it has been officially designated the American Band of the Supreme Allied Command. Its primary job is to broadcast to the A.E.F., and this is the job that arouses the enthusiasm of Glenn Miller himself and every man in his band. It is a job they have all been looking forward to, and one they all thoroughly enjoy. They will make a certain number of personal appearances at benefits and in hospitals for Allied Forces, but the first charge on their time and resources will be their broadcasts to you in your programme.

Every Thursday night Glenn Miller will conduct the full band in a half-hour broadcast (20.30-21.00 DBST) in which he will introduce famous British guest artists and visiting stars. This full band numbers forty players, and they include some of the finest players of American dance music. For instance : Drummer Sergeant Ray McKinley, who led his own band ; Sergeant Mel Powell, formerly pianist with Benny Goodman ; Sergeant Carmen Mastren, who played guitar with Tommy Dorsey ; Sergeant Bobby Nichols, whom swing fans will remember with Vaughn Munroe. Leading vocalist is Sergeant Johnny Desmond, who used to sing with Gene Krupa. By this time, those of you who have been able to listen will have discovered for yourselves what happens when a bunch of experts like this gets together in a big band with Glenn Miller in charge. The result is a band such as nobody heard in peacetime ; it is a weekly special performance for the A.E.F.

Strings of Famous American Symphony Orchestras

Besides the big show on Thursday nights, the talent that has come over with Glenn Miller will contribute several other special programmes to the A.E.F. Programme. On Tuesday at 20.05 you will hear broadcasts conducted by Ray McKinley, with a band comparable in make-up to the pre-war Glenn Miller band. On Monday and Wednesday at 19.45 there are fifteen-minute programmes by ' Strings with Wings,' a twenty-piece string band formed from the full band, including members of America's most famous symphony orchestras, and conducted by Sergeant George Ockner, who used to be concert-master with some of America's leading radio orchestras.

Watch for them in the programmes, and for other combinations like the swing sextet with Mel Powell at the piano, the string quartet, and Johnny Desmond's own programme of songs supported by the entire band.

From Combat Diary at one end of the scale to Glenn Miller's musicians at the other, the A.E.F. Programme plans to bring you new broadcasts of every type specially intended for you. It is your programme. Let us know what you think of it, what you like, and what you want—the address to write to is : The Director, Allied Expeditionary Forces Programme, BBC, London, W.1. Your letters will be a great help.

One other thing : the team that Glenn Miller has brought over is called ' The American Band of the Supreme Allied Command.' It will soon be joined by the British and Canadian Bands of the Supreme Allied Command. Watch the programmes for their first broadcasts.

Drummer Sgt. RAY McKINLEY, who led a famous peacetime band of his own

Sgt. MEL POWELL, formerly pianist with Benny Goodman

A.E.F. (pages 2, 4, and 20), HOME SERVICE, and GENERAL FORCES PROGRAMMES for the week

The AEF (Allied Expeditionary Forces) programme was operated by the BBC and began broadcasting 7th June 1944. It finished on 28th July 1945.

HEAVY
PARCELS
BY PASSENGER TRAIN
CAUSE
DELAY

OCTOBER 1944

SMALLER PARCELS — QUICKER DELIVERY

British Railways can take the strain of war because for years a large proportion of earnings went to maintaining a standard of efficiency which no other railway system in the world has equalled.

BRITISH RAILWAYS
GWR — LMS — LNER — SR

A Christmas Card from a Prisoner of War.

Central Avenue, Castle Bromwich Aeroplane Factory,
Kingsbury Road, 1945.

Grey's Bull Street, 1945.

A correspondent has suggested an all-night City Transport service.

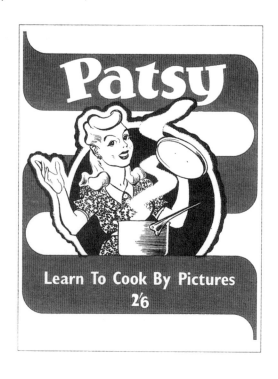

Ivor Novello appears in his musical, "The Dancing Years", Hippodrome, 15th January 1945. Roma Beaumont shares the piano stool and Mary Ellis looks down on them.

Major Charity Adams inspects her American Central Postal Battalion, February 1945. They later took part in a parade in the city.

Members of the Birmingham Philharmonic Orchestra, Central Hall, Corporation Street 1945.

HITLER DEAD

News the world's 2.5.45 been praying for broken last night by German radio

THE LAST PICTURE

TOP SECRET   TOP SECRET
SHAEF FORWARD

STAFF MESSAGE CONTROL
OUTGOING MESSAGE

T O P   S E C R E T

U R G E N T

TO   AGWAR FOR COMBINED CHIEFS OF STAFF,
           AMSSO FOR BRITISH CHIEFS OF STAFF

FROM   SHAEF FORWARD, SIGNED EISENHOWER

REF NO   FWD -20798   TOO: 070 325 B

SCAF 355

The mission of this Allied Force was
fulfilled at 0241, local time, May 7th, 1945.

EISENHOWER

ORIGINATOR   SUPREME COMMANDER   AUTHENTICATION: J B MOORE
                                               Lt Colonel

INFORMATION   : TO ALL GENERAL AND SPECIAL STAFF DIVISIONS

NAZIS SURRENDER
EUROPE WAR COMES 7/5/45 TO END

 LATE EXTRA

The Daily Sketch

 VICTORY PICTURE

No. 11,223 ★★ TUESDAY, MAY 8, 1945 A KEMSLEY NEWSPAPER ONE PENNY

THIS IS VE-DAY

Premier Is To Broadcast At 3p.m.: Two Days' Holiday

THE KING SAYS: Crushing Victory

VE Day, Lupin Street, Bloomsbury, 8th May 1945.

VE Day, Arthur Street, Small Heath, 8th May 1945.

HELP HIM
finish the Job

VOTE NATIONAL

NO MORE DOLE QUEUES.... SO IT'S
LABOUR
FOR SECURITY

VOTE LABOUR FOR SELF-RESPECTING JOBS LABOUR X

STATE OF PARTIES

GOVERNMENT	At Dissolution	To-day
Conservative ..	358	153
National	4	1
Lib.-National ..	27	12
Total	389	166
OPPOSITION		
Labour	168	311
Liberal	19	9
I.L.P.	3	2
Communist ..	1	1
Common Wealth	3	1
Independent ..	25	7
Total	219	331

Councillor Jim Simmons, Leader of the Birmingham Borough Labour Party, snapped at his hour of victory.

IN BIRMINGHAM, LABOUR WON NINE SEATS FROM THE CONSERVATIVES AND ALSO GAINED THE NEW SEAT AT ACOCK'S GREEN. EDGBASTON, MOSELEY AND HANDSWORTH ARE THE ONLY SEATS REMAINING TO THE CONSERVATVES IN THE ONE-TIME TORY STRONGHOLD. 26.7.45

53

CINEMATOGRAPH EXHIBITORS' ASSOCIATION

ADELPHI, HAY MILLS. (A.B.C.). VIC. 1208.—Raymond Massey, Hotel Berlin (a); Ann Miller, Eadie Was a Lady (a). Sunday: Girl Trouble (u).

ALBION, New Inns, HANDSWORTH.—MADONNA OF THE SEVEN MOONS (A). Phyllis Calvert. Full Support. Sunday: If I Were Boss (u), etc.

ALHAMBRA, Moseley-rd. VIC. 2826.—Cary Grant, ARSENIC & OLD LACE (a). Sunday: George Raft, Background to Danger (a), etc.

APOLLO, TYBURN-ROAD.—RONALD COLMAN, KISMET (U). Fine Support Programme. Sunday: Henry Fonda, Immortal Sergeant, a; Mad Martindales

ASTORIA, ASTON. (A.B.C.). AST. 2384 Jean Arthur, Lee Bowman, Impatient Years (a); Perilous Journey (a). Sunday: Dinner at The Ritz (u).

ATLAS, STECHFORD. STE. 2206.— Ronald Colman, Loretta Young, THE DEVIL TO PAY (U); EVERYTHING ON ICE (U). Sunday: Dr. Syn (a).

BEACON, Smethwick. (A.B.C.). SME. 1045.—James Cagney, G MEN (A); Gordon Harker, NO PARKING (A). Sun.: Loretta Young, CHINA (A).

BEACON, Great Barr (opp. Scott Arms). DARK WATERS (A). 2.15, 5.35, 9.0; HISTORY IS MADE AT NIGHT (A). 3.50, 7.15. Sun.: The £100 Window.

BEAUFORT, Washwood Heath—Nelson Eddy, Jeanette MacDonald, MAYTIME (U). Sunday: Pluck of the Irish (a). 25½ Hours' Leave (u).

BIRCHFIELD, Perry Barr. BIR. 4355. Greer Garson, Walter Pidgeon in Mrs. Parkington (a); The Memphis Belle (u) (Tech). Sun., 5.0: Spy Train (a).

BRISTOL, Bristol-road (A.B.C.). CAL. 1904. 2.0 till 11.0. — Laird Cregar, George Sanders, HANGOVER SQUARE (A); EVER SINCE VENUS (A).

BROADWAY, Bristol-street. MID. 1761. BOWERY TO BROADWAY (A); and MARSHAL OF GUNSMORE (U). Sun.: Isle of Missing Men (a).

CAPITOL.—A SONG TO REMEMBER (A). Technicolor, with Merle Oberon. Paul Muni, at 3.15, 5.45, 8.15. Sunday: THE PLAINSMAN (A).

CARLTON, SPARKBROOK. SOU. 0861. Deanna Durbin, Can't Help Singing (u) (Tech.); Noah Beery, Jun., Pass to Romance (u). Sun.: The Squeaker (a).

CASTLE BROMWICH CINEMA—Daily at 2.30—Edward G. Robinson, THE WOMAN IN THE WINDOW (A); Full Support. Sun.: Gung Ho (a).

CLIFTON, GREAT BARR.—The Cry of The Werewolf (a), 2.15, 4.35, 6.55, 9.15; Soul of a Monster (a), 3.35, 5.55, 8.15. Sunday: Happidrome (u).

CORONET, SMALL HEATH. VIC. 0420 Ray Milland in Reap The Wild Wind (a) (Technicolor). Sunday: Sherlock Holmes in Washington (u).

CROWN, Ladywood. (A.B.C.). Edg.1122. TARZAN'S SECRET TREASURE (U); ROAD SHOW (U). Sunday: Dr. Gillespie's New Assistant (a).

DANILO, LONGBRIDGE.—MAN IN HALF MOON STREET (A). 2.15, 5.20, 8.30; Ghost of St. Michael's (u), 4.0, 7.0. Sunday: Are Husbands Necessary?

DANILO, QUINTON.—EDDIE CANTOR in STRIKE ME PINK, 2.30, 5.27, 8.29; SHE WHO DARES, 3.53, 6.55. Monday: In the Meantime, Darling.

EDGBASTON, Monument-road (A.B.C.) Anton Walbrook, The Man from Morocco (a); When Strangers Marry (a). Sunday: Edge of Darkness (a).

ELITE, HANDSWORTH. NOR. 0665. JEAN PORTER, SAN FERNANDO VALLEY (U); MARY LEE in THREE LITTLE SISTERS (U).

EMPIRE, SMETHWICK. SME. 0757. Tito Guizar, Virginia Bruce in BRAZIL (U); also Bill Elliott in POWER OF JUSTICE (A).

EMPRESS, Sutton. (A.B.C.). Sut. 2365. Jeanette MacDonald, Nelson Eddy. Maytime (u). Sun.: Piccadilly Round About (u). Sun.: Keeper of the Flame (a).

ERA CINEMA, BORDESLEY GREEN. Stewart Granger in Waterloo Road (a); Twilight On The Prairie (u). Sunday: The Silver Fleet.

GAIETY, Coleshill-st. (A.B.C.). Cen. 6649. — Ronald Colman, Marlene Dietrich, KISMET (U) (Tech.). Sun.: Appointment in Berlin (u).

GLOBE, ASTON. AST. 0652.—SOUTH RIDING (U). Ralph Richardson; RAWHIDE (U). Sunday: Clancy Street Boys (u); Prison Mutiny (a).

GRAND, Soho-road, HANDSWORTH.—Casanova in Burlesque (u), Joe E. Brown; Deerslayer (u), Jean Parker. Sunday: Hitting the Headlines (u).

GRAND, Alum Rock-road, SALTLEY.—DARK VICTORY (A). BETTE DAVIS and GEORGE BRENT. SUNDAY: HURRICANE SMITH (A).

GRANGE, SMALL HEATH. VIC. 0434. Cary Grant, Ethel Barrymore in None But The Lonely Heart (a); Full Sup.. Sun.: Sherlock Holmes Faces Death (a)

GROVE CINEMA, Dudley-rd. SME. 0343 The Thin Man Goes Home (a), Thurs. and Fri., 3.21, 5.52, 8.23, Sat. 3.50, 6.21, 8.47. Sun: Old Mother Riley, M.P.

IMPERIAL, Moseley-road. (A.B.C.) Cal. 2283.—Eddie Cantor, KID MILLIONS (A); Anna Neagle, NELL GWYN (A). Sun.: Dr. Gillespie's New Assistant (a).

KING'S NORTON. KIN. 1079.—Fri. 5.0, Sat. 4.15. Alexander Knox, Geraldine Fitzgerald, in WILSON (U) (Tech.). Sunday: SHIP AHOY (U).

KINGSTON, SMALL HEATH. VIC. 2639 Greer Garson, Walter Pidgeon in MRS. PARKINGTON (A). Sunday: When the Daltons Rode (a).

KINGSWAY. HIG. 1352.—HANGOVER SQUARE (A), Laird Cregar, Linda Darnell, George Sanders; Tahiti Nights (a). Sunday: Neutral Port (u), etc.

LUXOR.—VIRGINIA BRUCE, TITO GUIZAR in BRAZIL (U); also OUTLAWS OF STAMPEDE PASS. Sun.: Rookies (u), Abbott & Costello.

LYRIC.—Ray Milland, John Wayne in REAP THE WILD WIND (a), glorious Technicolor, etc. Sun.: Return of the Scarlet Pimpernel (u), Desert Phantom

MAJESTIC — — — SMETHWICK Mervyn Johns and Lesley Brook in TWILIGHT HOUR (U); Laurel and Hardy in AIR RAID WARDENS (U).

MAYFAIR — — PERRY COMMON Constance Moore. ATLANTIS CITY (U); PISTOL PACKIN' MAMA (U) Sunday: Call of the Yukon (u).

MAYPOLE, King's Heath. WAR. 2051. Fri. Sat. at 5.0. Ronald Colman in CYNARA (U); Bobby Breen in LET'S SING AGAIN (U). Sunday: Q Planes.

NORTHFIELD CINEMA.—Greer Garson and Walter Pidgeon in MRS. PARKINGTON (A). Cont. from 6 p.m. Sunday: Capt. Fury (a); A Chump at Oxford (u)

OAK, SELLY OAK. (A.B.C.). Sel. 0139. Jeanette MacDonald, Nelson Eddy, MAYTIME (U). Sunday: THREE HEARTS FOR JULIA (A).

ODEON, KINGSTANDING. SUT. 2551. Phyllis Calvert, MADONNA OF THE SEVEN MOONS (A); also Animal Wonderland. Sun. 5: Captain Fury (a)

ODEON, PERRY BARR. BIR. 4455. Continuous 2.0. THE SUSPECT (A). Also THE GHOST CATCHERS (A). Sunday: STAGECOACH (U).

ODEON, SHIPLEY. SHI. 1165. Cont 1.0—10.0. GUEST IN THE HOUSE (A). Also SHE GETS HER MAN (A). Sunday: Chump at Oxford (u)

ODEON ...... SUTTON COLDFIELD NONE BUT THE LONELY HEART (A), Cary Grant, Ethel Barrymore. Sun.: Janet Gaynor, Young in Heart (A)

ODEON, WARLEY—CARY GRANT in NONE BUT THE LONELY HEART (A), 1.30; 4.40, 7.55 p.m. Also SWING OUT, SISTER (T).

OLTON CINEMA—Nils Asther, THE MAN IN HALF MOON STREET (A). TAKE IT BIG (T). Sunday: Bing Crosby, We're Not Dressing (u)

OLYMPIA, Ladypool-road. VIC. 0124. CASANOVA IN BURLESQUE (T). Joe Brown: DEER SLAYER (T), Jean Paris Calling (a); Sing Another Chorus

ORIENT, ASTON. (A.R.C). Nor 1815 Anton Walbrook, The Man from Morocco (a); When Strangers Marry (a). Sunday: Ghost Breakers (a)

PALACE, Erdington. (A.B.C.). Ero 1722 Jeanette MacDonald, Nelson Eddy, MAYTIME (T). Sunday: Flanagan and Allen. THEATRE ROYAL (T)

PALLADIUM, Hockley. (A.R.C.) No 0390.—Joel McCrea, Barbara Stanwyck John Garrick, Broken Melody (u). Sun.: Andy Hardy's Double Life (u)

PAVILION, Stirchley. (A.B.C.). Kin. 1241.—Walbrook-Scott, The Man from Morocco (a); When Strangers Marry (a). Sun.: The Ghost Breakers (a)

PAVILION, Wylde Green. (A.B.C.). Erd 0224.—Anton Walbrook, THE MAN FROM MOROCCO (A). Sunday: Errol Flynn, Edge of Darkness (a)

PICCADILLY, Sparkbrook (A.B.C.) Vic. 1688.—Anne Baxter, Ralph Bellamy, Guest In The House (a). Sun.: Edge of Darkness (a)

PICTURE HOUSE (G.B.). HARBORNE DAVID NIVEN, PAUL LUKAS in DODSWORTH (A). 3.10, 5.50, 8.30 Also BORDER PATROL (U).

PLAZA, Stockland Green. ERD. 1552. Joan Davies, SHE GETS HER MAN (A); Bob Crosby, SINGING SHERIFF (U). Sun.: There Goes My Heart (u)

PRINCES, SMETHWICK. SME. 0221. Margaret O'Brien, Jimmy Durante in MUSIC FOR MILLIONS (A). Sunday: Ladies In Retirement (a), etc.

REGAL, Handsworth. (A.B.C.). Nor 1801.—Anton Walbrook, The Man from Morocco (a); When Strangers Marry (a) Last pro. 6.45. Sun.: Happy Go Lucky

RIALTO, HALL GREEN. SPR. 1270. MADONNA OF THE SEVEN MOONS (A). Phyllis Calvert, Stewart Granger. Full Support. Sunday: Plunder (u).

RINK (G.B.), SMETHWICK. SME. 0950. Continuous 2—10. BETTE DAVIS in JEZEBEL (A); Johnny Mack Brown, PARTNERS OF THE TRAIL (A).

RITZ, Bordesley Green, E. (A.B.C.). Vic. 1070.—Faye Emerson, HOTEL BERLIN (A); EADIE WAS A LADY (A). Sun.: So Ends Our Night (a).

ROBIN HOOD, Hall Green. (A.B.C.). SPR. 2371.—The Man from Morocco (a); When Strangers Marry (a). Sun.: Footlight Serenade (u).

ROCK CINEMA, ALUM ROCK. Free Car Park.—Alexander Knox in WILSON (U) (Tech.). Full Support. Sun.: One Hundred Pound Window.

ROYALTY, Harborne. (A.B.C.). HAR 1619.—Anton Walbrook. The Man from Morocco (a); When Strangers Marry (a). Sun: Background to Danger

RUBERY CINEMA, PHONE 193.— Gary Cooper, Teresa Wright, Casanova Brown (a); Sons of the Air (u). Sunday: CAPTAIN FURY (U).

SAVOY, KING'S NORTON. KIN. 1069. Tom Conway, THE FALCON IN MEXICO (A); PERILOUS JOURNEY (A). Sun.: Millions Like Us (u).

SHELDON CINEMA, SHE. 2158.— EDDIE CANTOR in KID MILLIONS (A). Sunday: We Dive at Dawn (u); Eyes of the Underworld (a)

SOLIHULL (SOL. 0393).—CHARLES LAUGHTON, MAUREEN O'HARA in JAMAICA INN (A). Sunday: First Love (u); Hit the Road (a).

STAR CINEMA—Atlantic City (u), Constance Moore, 3.40, 6.20, 8.55; Pistol Packin' Mama (a). Sunday: San Francisco (a), Clark Gable.

TIVOLI PLAYHOUSE, Coventry-road— Gary Cooper, Laraine Day, THE STORY OF DR. WASSELL (A) (Tech.). Sun.: Honeymoon Lodge (u)

TRIANGLE, Gooch-street. CAL. 1069. Everything On Ice (u), Irena Dare; Mystery of Mr. Wong (u). Sunday: Ghosts In The Night (u).

TUDOR, King's Heath. (A.B.C.). HIG. 1151.—Spencer Tracy, Van Johnson. THIRTY SECONDS OVER TOKIO (A). Sun.: Commandos Strike at Dawn.

VICTORIA, EAS. 0479. — THESE THREE (A), Merle Oberon; THE CHINESE CAT (A), Sidney Toler. Sunday: Face Behind The Mask (a).

VILLA CROSS (G.B.). NOR. 0607.— EDDIE CANTOR in KID MILLIONS (A); also ROAD SHOW (U). Sunday: QUEEN OF SPIES (U).

WARWICK CINEMA, Acock's Green. Lon Chaney and Jean Parker, DEAD MAN'S EYES (A); NIGHT CLUB GIRL (U). Sun.: Crime Smasher (a).

WEOLEY, WEOLEY CASTLE. Cont. from 5.45.—SECRET COMMAND (A), Pat O'Brien; STARS ON PARADE (T). Sun.: Remember Pearl Harbour, u

WINDSOR, SMETHWICK. BEA. 2244. THE THIN MAN GOES HOME (A); Full Supporting Programme. Sunday: Lone Wolf Takes a Chance (a), etc.

WINSON GREEN. NORthern 1790.— STORM OVER LISBON (A), Vera Ralston; PISTOL PACKIN' MAMA (A). Sunday: Trade Winds (a), etc.

WEST BROMWICH CINEMAS

CLIFTON, STONE CROSS. STO. 2141. THE IMPATIENT YEARS (A), 3.14, 6.0, 8.54; Dangerous Mists (a), 1.55, 4.55, 7.49. Sun: Saint in Palm Springs

IMPERIAL, West Bromwich. WES. 0192 BOWERY TO BROADWAY (A). Also NIGHT CLUB GIRL (U). Sunday: Leslie Banks, 21 DAYS (U).

PALACE CINEMA, WES. 0358. WINGED VICTORY (U), featuring the American Air Force. Full Support. Sunday: Made for Each Other (a).

PLAZA, WEST BROMWICH. WES. 0030 SAN FERNANDO VALLEY (U). Also PORT OF FORTY THIEVES (a). Sun.: Man who could Work Miracles, a

QUEEN'S CINEMA. WES. 0351. Flanagan & Allen in DREAMING, COMEDY, NEWS, and INTEREST. Sun.: TUTTLES OF TAHITI.

ST. GEORGE'S CINEMA, Phone 0737. Phyllis Calvert and Stewart Granger. FANNY BY GASLIGHT. Sunday: SHE GOT HER MAN.

TOWER. (A.B.C.).. WES. 1210.— Judy Garland, Robert Walker, Under the Clock (a); The Great Mike Sun.: Happy Go Lucky (u).

MISCELLANEOUS.

An extra hour?

THE Brewers' Association has not yet considered whether any applications should be made to the Justices for an extension of hours for the official holiday.

When Germany was knocked out of the war the Government suggested local licensing authorities should give sympathetic consideration to any application for a little extra conviviality, and in Birmingham the public-houses were open an hour extra on the night of VE-day.

Given the same encouragement from Whitehall the Birmingham Licensing Bench will no doubt be equally sympathetic to any application which the Brewers' Association might decide to make.

So far as theatres and cinemas are concerned the whole position has changed since then. Special applications had to be made for longer hours of opening on VE-day, but the emergency restrictions have all been withdrawn since then and places of entertainment are back to their pre-war liberties.

TRAINS CROWDED— ALL AWAY

" VERY, very good. Everyone got away." That was how the situation at the Birmingham stations was described to-day.

All the trains were crowded, but not unduly so. The biggest crowds appeared to be for the West of England—Blackpool not being in so great a demand as it has during past weeks.

There were plenty of extra trains, and they were not all even filled. The 7.14 from New-street Station to the North had extra coaches put on which were not needed.

Passengers from Victoria Station, London, to-day, found reaching their trains "easy as A.B.C." under the new alphabetical queue system. Although many more people are travelling now the station was far less congested than it was by earlier holiday-makers.

At Paddington Station a loudspeaker was used to direct crowds queueing outside. Four extra trains were put on for Exeter and Torquay, Newport, and Cardiff, and several other trains duplicated.

While mounted police were controlling the crowds at Paddington, Euston was experiencing little difficulty with queues. Trains for stations to Holyhead and Llandudno were crowded, but no one was left behind.

Six extra trains were put on for Manchester, Blackpool, Liverpool, and Llandudno.

WEEK-END Public Opinion

SIR.—Where did all the tomatoes go last week? I read in the paper that plenty of tomatoes were coming from Jersey and thought I should be able to walk straight to a shop and get some.

Did I? After waiting an hour in the queue I got none at all. After standing an hour the following morning I got nine shillings' worth, however.

We women are just fed up with queues and more so on this estate, as there are not enough shops. I don't know how we shall get on when we have those 200 houses finished. QUEUE WEARY
Lea Hall.

Hard riding

LAST Sunday I went by charabanc to visit my sister who is ill at Salterley Grange, Cheltenham. After waiting 1½ hours the vehicle turned out to be a "utility," with hard wooden seats, and four had to stand all the way.

If this is the best that can be done for the public visiting sick people, it's time war prisoners were made to ride in them, or, failing this, as Salterley Grange is a Birmingham institution, why cannot the authorities organise these trips? People should be allowed to book seats, not have to wait about. FORWARD.

Kingstanding.

Daisy Day

THE amount received in connection with Daisy Day to date, including donations, is just under £1,800. We are hoping that the final figure will greatly exceed this.

If any who have been unable to send their usual donation will be good enough to do so, through the Princess Alice Orphanage, the gift will be gratefully acknowledged by GEORGE F. SMITH.
Birmingham 3.

Prize-winners in the L.M.S. Parcels Horse Parade in Queen's Drive to-day. They are: J. Harper, with Stocky; J. Wale, with Willie; and L. W. Williams, with Robin.

Evening Despatch

Gazette Buildings, B'ham.

'Grams:
Evening Despatch, B'ham.

'Phone:
Central 8461 (15 lines).

Japan at Potsdam

SOMETHING IS ABOUT TO HAPPEN in connection with the war in the Far East, especially in Japan.

It is too much to expect collapse or immediate surrender, but unless the signs are camouflage, for which there would be no excuse, they indicate a changed attitude in Tokio.

Else, why was Lord Louis Mountbatten, our commander in South-east Asia, at Berlin?

This is a piquant disclosure, accentuated by the unofficial statement that he was diverted from Cairo when on his way to London.

The incident is all the more interesting in coinnciding with reports that there have been some sort of talks between Japanese and Russian emissaries and that Japan has thrown out a definite demand for better terms than unconditional surrender.

EACH in itself is significant. In combination, they look like a portent.

That Japan is getting tired of the war and is no longer hopeful of victory, or even stalemate, is a conclusion that would be sensible, if we could gauge the subtleties of the oriental mind.

A fanatical policy of defence by suicide sounds to us like madness, and it would not be surprising if Japan, which has prided itself for decades on having studied Western ways and to have improved upon them, is beginning to take the same view.

Her Air Force has been well-nigh put out of action, and now her navy lies crippled. Her principal cities, with their factories, and her harbours are being ceaselessly bombed; and she cannot close her eyes to the terribly destructive efficacy of the Allied bombing of Germany.

Moscow says "unconditional surrender" is plain enough

END OF THE WAR: "SOME HOURS" DELAY

EISENHOWER FOR MOSCOW

AN American broadcast from Moscow to-day said Gen. Eisenhower, former Supreme Commander on the Western Front, is expected in Moscow at any moment.

The broadcast, by Eddy Gilmore of the N.B.C., said that the general is going to the U.S.S.R. not on business but on pleasure as a guest of the Russians.

Big Four in high-speed talks on the Mikado issue

U.S. has drafted a reply

Attlee, at midnight, gives news that the war is over

PEACE ON EARTH

*Japs reply: We have the honour to surrender.
Mikado orders all Forces to cease fire*

VJ celebrations outside the Council House, 15th August 1945.

Sports Quiz No. 2

1 What is the longest distance ever travelled by a cyclist in 1 hour?

2 "Dixie" Dean was (a) scrum-half (b) centre-half (c) centre-forward?

3 Which famous bowler once took 10 wickets for 10 runs?

4 Which was the most popular tennis racket at Wimbledon before the war?

Answers

1 L. Vandersuyft cycled 76 miles, 503 yards in 1 hour (paced).

2 Centre-forward.

3 Hedley Verity.

4 Dunlop, of course.

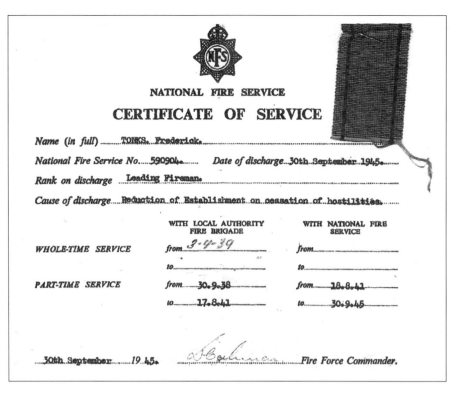

Paul Schofield appears in three plays at Birmingham Repertory Theatre, Station Street, 1945. He was born in Birmingham in 1922 and was made a Companion of Honour in 2001. He actually turned down a knighthood.

Noelle Gordon appeared at the Alexandra Theatre in "Cinderella", Christmas 1944 and "Dick Whittington", 1945. She later found fame as "Meg Richardson" in TV's "Crossroads".

"Travelling Around" was a promotional film made by the British Film Institute, in 1945, to promote the city to potential visitors.

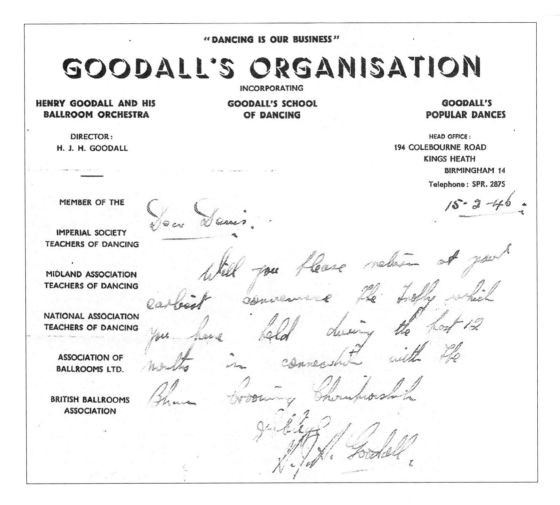

"DANCING IS OUR BUSINESS"

GOODALL'S ORGANISATION

INCORPORATING

HENRY GOODALL AND HIS BALLROOM ORCHESTRA	GOODALL'S SCHOOL OF DANCING	GOODALL'S POPULAR DANCES

DIRECTOR:
H. J. H. GOODALL

HEAD OFFICE:
194 COLEBOURNE ROAD
KINGS HEATH
BIRMINGHAM 14
Telephone: SPR. 2875

MEMBER OF THE

IMPERIAL SOCIETY
TEACHERS OF DANCING

MIDLAND ASSOCIATION
TEACHERS OF DANCING

NATIONAL ASSOCIATION
TEACHERS OF DANCING

ASSOCIATION OF
BALLROOMS LTD.

BRITISH BALLROOMS
ASSOCIATION

15-3-46

Dear Davis,

Will you please return at your earliest convenience the trophy which you have held during the last 12 months in connection with the Blue Crooning Championship.

Yours,
H. J. H. Goodall.

The main entrance to the University of Birmingham buildings, Edgbaston, 1946.

Ludgate Hill, with Great Charles Street on the left, 1946.

A lot of fruit and vegetables were in short supply after the war, 1946.

Birmingham City

DIVISION 2 CHAMPIONS
Back:- D.Fairhurst (Trainer), K.Green, E.Duckhouse, G.Merrick, F.Mitchell, D.Jennings
Front:- J.Stewart, C.Dougall, F.Harris, H.Storer (Manager), C.Trigg, H.Bodle, G.Edwards.

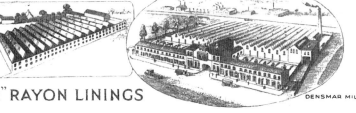

Comedian, Sid Field, stars in the film, "London Town", 1946. He was born in Ladywood in 1904 but lived in Osborn Road, Sparkbrook, for most of his early life.

"Ignorance Is Bliss", starring Harold Berens, Stewart MacPherson, Gladys Hay and Michael Moore, was a BBC radio programme that began in April 1946.

Recording "Itma", one of the most popular radio programmes of the forties, are Tony Francis, Deryck Guyler, Molly Weir and Tommy Handley, 1946.

Metropole cinema, Snow Hill, 1946. Originally known as The New Star, it closed after twice suffering bomb damage.

New Street Station, 1946.

After six years without county cricket, season 1946 saw the County Championship start again. Peter Cramner came back from the Army to lead the side. Team group for 1946. Standing (left to right) Eric Hollies, Bill Fantham, Tom Dollery, "Tiger" Smith (coach), M. Barker, Ken Taylor (now Cricket Manager of Nottinghamshire), Norman Shortland and Jimmy Ord. Sitting (left to right), R. Mead-Briggs, C. S. Dempster (New Zealand Test player), Peter Cramner (captain), Cyril Goodway (now Chairman of the club), and Charles Adderley.

Queen's Head Steelhouse Lane, 1946.

65

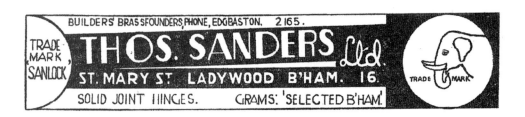

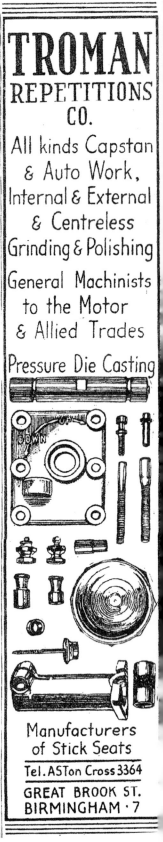

67

Woolworths' staff party, Shirley Road, Acocks Green, Christmas 1946.

From High Street, leading down into the Bull Ring, January 1947.

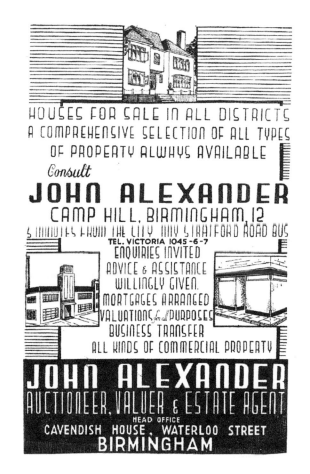

Aubrey Road, with Digby Park, showing the park keeper's hut, Small Heath, c 1947.

Dovedale Road, Perry Common, c 1947.

Baskerville House (The Civic Centre), 1947.

Help with the work on a coal barge, c 1947.

Slade Road, Erdington, 1947.

"Old Mother Riley and Her Daughter" (Arthur Lucan and Kitty McShane) Hippodrome, 29th May 1947.

The News Theatre, High Street, c 1947.

Hazel Court, one of the stars of "Holiday Camp", 1947. She was born in Birmingham, in 1926, and her family moved to Sutton Coldfield six months later.

GPO Stores, Fordrough Lane, Bordesley Green 1947.

A Selection of

MINISTRY OF FOOD PUBLICATIONS

THE MANUAL OF NUTRITION
(New Edition, 1947)

Sets out the elementary principles of nutrition for students and others who need a sound basic knowledge of the subject.

Price **1**s. *By post* 1s. 2d.

FOOD AND NUTRITION
(Every fourth week)

A topical periodical of particular interest to teachers and students in domestic science colleges.

Price **3**d. *By post* 4d.

Or 12 issues for 4s.

THE A.B.C. OF COOKERY
(Revised 1947)

A complete guide to the housewife, particularly in time of food restrictions. It covers shopping, food storage, cookery methods and meal planning, but is not a recipe book.

Price **1**s. *By post* 1s. 2d.

FISH COOKERY

Buying and choosing fish : Preparation for cooking : Methods of cooking and serving : A number of interesting and useful recipes.

Price **6**d. *By post* 7d.

Obtainable from

H.M. STATIONERY OFFICE

The Public Bar of the New Inns, Holyhead Road, Handsworth, c 1947.

Ladywood Road, from Monument Road, 1947.

Final year dental students, QE Hospital, 1947.

Corporation Street, 1947.

New Street/Bennetts Hill, c 1947. Grosvenor House was finally completed in 1955.

Roy Dillon meets Father Christmas, Lewis's,
November 1947.

Coventry Road, Small Heath, November 1947.

Preaching the gospel, just across from the Market Hall, Bull Ring, 1947.

A classroom at Selly Oak Hospital, c 1947.

Preparing for the Birmingham University Rag Week, November 1947. The humorous poster, "Trips To The Sound Barrier", refers to the fact that George Welch had unofficially broken the speed record the month before.

ALEXANDRA THEATRE

JOHN BRIGHT STREET AND STATION STREET
BIRMINGHAM

Managing Director and Licensee - - - DEREK SALBERG
Directors: BASIL THOMAS, J. THOMAS, S. THOMAS, C. KEELING, G. C. KING
General Manager - - - - - W. A. DOBSON
Secretary and Accountant - - - - C. WOOLDRIDGE

Tele No.—MID. 1231

| EVENINGS AT 7·0 | MATINEES AT 2·0 |

Derek Salberg's

1947-48 PANTOMIME

BABES IN THE WOOD

BOX OFFICE OPEN 10 a.m. to 7-15 p.m.   Telephone : MID. 1231

BABES IN THE WOOD

THE CHARACTERS IN THE PANTOMIME
(IN ORDER OF APPEARANCE)

ROBIN HOOD	LISA LEE
FRIAR TUCK	NEVILLE MAPP
LABOURER	EUNICE HINSLEY
JOHNNY GREEN	RAF
THE SHERIFF OF NOTTINGHAM	JACK ELMONT
DAME TROT	TOMMY JOVER
MAID MARIAN	HERMENE FRENCH
BIG BEN	COLIN LAURENCE
WILL SCARLET } Robin	OLIVER HARDWICKE
ALAN-A-DALE } Hood's	WYNN DYSON
LITTLE JOHN } Men	MICHAEL LANGDON
MUCH THE MILLER'S SON	KENNETH DOUGHTY
LITTLE BILLY	EDDIE CONNOR
PETER } The	BRENDA JAGGER
PAULINE } Babes	SHEILA JAGGER
(By arrangement with RICH BELLAIRS School of Dancing)	
CUTHBERT (The Babes's Dog)	GEORGE HURST
FAIRY STARLIGHT	JUDITH WHITAKER
JACK IN THE BOX	RAF
PERSIAN CAT }	FAITH
GIPSY GIRL }	
YE DOGGIES	DUNCAN'S COLLIES
SID THE SPIV	RAF
CREEPY (a gnome)	GEORGE HURST
GRIZZLY (a bear)	BERYL PAGE
KING RICHARD COEUR DE LION	NEVILLE MAPP
LEHMISKI LADIES ::	ALEXANDRA BABES

SYLVESTER & NEPHEW

ACT ONE

SCENE 1	THE VILLAGE OF SHERWOOD
SCENE 2	THE SHERIFF'S BACKYARD
SCENE 3	THE VILLAGE SCHOOL
SCENE 4	OUTSIDE THE CITY WALLS
SCENE 5	THE NIGHT NURSERY
SCENE 6	CHRISTMAS LAND

ACT TWO

SCENE 7	NOTTINGHAM GOOSE FAIR
SCENE 8	ON THE WAY TO THE FOREST
SCENE 9	THE HAUNTED COTTAGE
SCENE 10	DEEPER IN THE FOREST
SCENE 11	THE GALLOWS OAK IN SHERWOOD FOREST
SCENE 12	ANOTHER PART OF THE FOREST
SCENE 13	THE TOWER
SCENE 14	A BARNYARD NEAR NOTTINGHAM CASTLE
SCENE 15	THE GREAT HALL AT NOTTINGHAM CASTLE

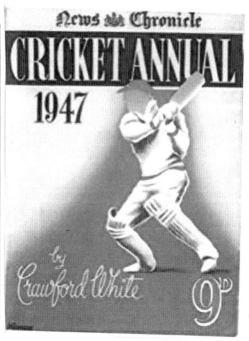

1948

January 1948

Sun	Mon	Tue	Wed	Thu	Fri	Sat
				1	2	3
4	5	6	7	8	9	10
11	12	13	14	15	16	17
18	19	20	21	22	23	24
25	26	27	28	29	30	31

February 1948

Sun	Mon	Tue	Wed	Thu	Fri	Sat
1	2	3	4	5	6	7
8	9	10	11	12	13	14
15	16	17	18	19	20	21
22	23	24	25	26	27	28
29						

March 1948

Sun	Mon	Tue	Wed	Thu	Fri	Sat
	1	2	3	4	5	6
7	8	9	10	11	12	13
14	15	16	17	18	19	20
21	22	23	24	25	26	27
28	29	30	31			

April 1948

Sun	Mon	Tue	Wed	Thu	Fri	Sat
				1	2	3
4	5	6	7	8	9	10
11	12	13	14	15	16	17
18	19	20	21	22	23	24
25	26	27	28	29	30	

May 1948

Sun	Mon	Tue	Wed	Thu	Fri	Sat
						1
2	3	4	5	6	7	8
9	10	11	12	13	14	15
16	17	18	19	20	21	22
23	24	25	26	27	28	29
30	31					

June 1948

Sun	Mon	Tue	Wed	Thu	Fri	Sat
		1	2	3	4	5
6	7	8	9	10	11	12
13	14	15	16	17	18	19
20	21	22	23	24	25	26
27	28	29	30			

July 1948

Sun	Mon	Tue	Wed	Thu	Fri	Sat
				1	2	3
4	5	6	7	8	9	10
11	12	13	14	15	16	17
18	19	20	21	22	23	24
25	26	27	28	29	30	31

August 1948

Sun	Mon	Tue	Wed	Thu	Fri	Sat
1	2	3	4	5	6	7
8	9	10	11	12	13	14
15	16	17	18	19	20	21
22	23	24	25	26	27	28
29	30	31				

September 1948

Sun	Mon	Tue	Wed	Thu	Fri	Sat
			1	2	3	4
5	6	7	8	9	10	11
12	13	14	15	16	17	18
19	20	21	22	23	24	25
26	27	28	29	30		

October 1948

Sun	Mon	Tue	Wed	Thu	Fri	Sat
					1	2
3	4	5	6	7	8	9
10	11	12	13	14	15	16
17	18	19	20	21	22	23
24	25	26	27	28	29	30
31						

November 1948

Sun	Mon	Tue	Wed	Thu	Fri	Sat
	1	2	3	4	5	6
7	8	9	10	11	12	13
14	15	16	17	18	19	20
21	22	23	24	25	26	27
28	29	30				

December 1948

Sun	Mon	Tue	Wed	Thu	Fri	Sat
			1	2	3	4
5	6	7	8	9	10	11
12	13	14	15	16	17	18
19	20	21	22	23	24	25
26	27	28	29	30	31	

www.thepeoplehistory.com

L.M.& S.R. For conditions see Back
MONTHLY RETURN
Valid One Month
BIRMINGHAM
(New Street)
TO
(EO
N'THAMPTON (CAS
THIRD CLASS
Fare 13/10 Z
4619

this Christmas
... give her a
Stratton
THE COMPACT FEATURING
THE SELF-OPENING INNER LID
Compact illustrated is in Engine Turned and Block Enamel finish No. 587 E.T.L. Price 50/-. In all-over Gilt Engine Turned finish No. 586 E.T. 60/-
A LARGE NUMBER OF EXQUISITE DESIGNS FOR YOUR CHOICE
Manufacturers: Jarrett, Rainsford & Laughton, Ltd., Kent Street, Birmingham.

SCHEDULE OF WAGE RATES AS AT JANUARY 1st, 1948

JOURNEYMEN ELECTRICIANS

	Hourly Basic Rate	*Temporary Hourly Addition*	*Hourly Inclusive Rate*
	s. d.	d.	s. d.
GRADE "A" AREA..	2 4	9	3 1
MERSEY DISTRICT	2 1½	9	2 10½
GRADE "B" AREAS	2 0½	9	2 9½

ADULT MATES :—

(In all cases adult mates are entitled to the full "Addition")

		s. d.		s. d.
BRISTOL ..	(80% of Jny'man's basic rate of	2 0½)	+9d. addition	=2 4½. per hr.
LONDON ..	(80% ,, ,, ,, ,, ,,	2 4)	+9d. ,,	=2 7½ ,,
OTHER AREAS	(75% ,, ,, ,, ,, ,,	2 0½)	+9d. ,,	=2 3½ ,,

MALE LABOUR UNDER 21 YEARS OF AGE (Categories II and III)

	Grade "A" hourly rate	*Grade "B" hourly rate*	*Mersey Dist. hourly rate*
Category II	s. d.	s. d.	s. d.
Age 16 (19 per cent. of J'nyman's rate)	0 5¼	0 4¾	0 5
Age 17 (25 ,, ,,)	0 7	0 6¼	0 6½
Age 18 (30 ,, ,,)	0 8½	0 7¼	0 7¾
Age 19 (45 ,, ,,)	1 0¼	0 11	0 11½
Age 20 (60 ,, ,,)	1 4¾	1 2¾	1 3¼
Category III.			
Age 16 (25 ,, ,,)	0 7	0 6¼	0 6½
Age 17 (35 ,, ,,)	0 9¾	0 8½	0 9
Age 18 (40 ,, ,,)	0 11¼	0 9¾	0 10¼
Age 19 (55 ,, ,,)	1 3½	1 1½	1 2
Age 20 (70 ,, ,,)	1 7½	1 5¼	1 5¾

To these rates is to be added a Temporary Hourly Addition as follows :—
To Labour under 18 years of age .. .. 3d. per hour
To Labour between 18 and 21 years of age .. .. .. 6d. per hour

Arthur Street Depot, Coventry Road, Small Heath, 1948.

Mill Lane, Northfield, 1948.

Austin A40s ready for distribution, Longbridge Works, Austin Motor Co. Ltd., 1948.

WHO'LL KILL INFLATION?

"**I**" says John Bull,
    "I speak for the nation—
We'll work with a will
    And we'll thus kill Inflation."

WHO'LL STRIKE THE FIRST BLOW?
"I," says the Director,
    "I'll keep prices low
And dividends down—
    I'll strike the first blow."

WHO'LL SEE IT DIE?
"I," says the Housewife,
    "For if I don't buy
Things I don't really need,
    Then I'll soon see it die."

WHO'LL RING THE BELL?
"I," says the worker,
    "I'll make more to sell
And not ask for a rise
    Till I <u>have</u> rung the bell!"

WHO'LL BE CHIEF MOURNER?
"I," says the Spiv,
    "If I can't make a 'corner'
In goods that are short,
    Then I'll be chief mourner."

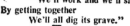

WHO'LL DIG ITS GRAVE?
"We," say the people,
    "We'll work and we'll save
By getting together
    We'll <u>all</u> dig its grave."

☀ **Credit Column**

THE Electric Lamp Manufacturers' Association, representing most of the industry, have reduced prices of electric bulbs by 5% to 12% according to size.

SAINSBURY'S home counties grocers, have reduced prices of certain foodstuffs by 6% to 25%. All Jaeger non-utility woollen clothing prices have dropped 10%.

"SOMETHING DONE"
Fully illustrated, it describes some post-war achievements of the British people. It is on sale at booksellers everywhere, 1/6.

TUBE Investments engineering group have reduced prices of electrically welded tubes by 2¼%. By introducing new managerial methods they have increased production in many of their factories.

—— Issued by His Majesty's Government. ——

Bull Ring, March 1948.

MACHINE TOOL MANUFACTURERS, ETC.
JAMES ARCHDALE AND CO. L^TD
MANCHESTER WORKS, LEDSAM ST. BIRMINGHAM

James Archdale & Co. Ltd., Ledsam Street, Ladywood, c 1948.

Here's the vitamin C and sugar they need

The surest way to get the Vitamin C and sugar lacking from to-day's food is from Scott & Turner's Rose Hip Syrup. It was made especially for this purpose, using rose hips rich in Vitamin C, plus sugar syrup — for energy. You need Vitamin C for vitality, to resist infection, to clear the skin and for healthy bones, gums and teeth. Take Scott & Turner's Rose Hip Syrup by the spoonful, or on porridge, cereal, ice cream, milk dishes and in fruit drinks. 1/9d. bottles, chemists only.

FOR ADULTS, TOO. ESPECIALLY NURSING & EXPECTANT MOTHERS

SCOTT & TURNER'S ROSE HIP SYRUP

Puts the roses in their cheeks

Mrs Ebourne outside her shop/cafe, Alexandra Street/Shakespeare Road, Ladywood, 1948.

Class 6, Camden Street School, Brookfields, 1948. The teachers are Miss Davies (left) and Miss Bagley.

Reading Room, Small Heath Library, Green Lane, c 1948. This was where Alton, as a small boy, developed his love for reading.

FAMILY GUIDE TO THE

National Insurance

SCHEME

The Scheme comes into full operation on

5th JULY 1948

PREPARED BY THE CENTRAL OFFICE OF INFORMATION FOR THE MINISTRY OF NATIONAL INSURANCE AND PUBLISHED BY HIS MAJESTY'S STATIONERY OFFICE

Your new National Health Service begins on 5th July. What is it? How do you get it?

It will provide you with all medical, dental, and nursing care. Everyone—rich or poor, man, woman or child—can use it or any part of it. There are no charges, except for a few special items. There are no insurance qualifications. But it is not a "charity". You are all paying for it, mainly as taxpayers, and it will relieve your money worries in time of illness.

The Tea Rooms, Victoria Park, Coventry Road, Small Heath, c 1948.

Kings Norton Grammar School Old Boys' cricket team
("The Old Nortonians") 1948.

Don Bradman, bowled for a duck by Warwickshire leg break bowler, Eric Hollies, in his last test match at the Oval, 14th August 1948. Four more runs and he would have averaged 100 in Test Cricket.

Alan Napier, born in Kings Norton in 1903, found fame portraying Alfred the butler in the TV series, "Batman". In 1948 he was one of the stars of "Macbeth". He was a cousin of Neville Chamberlain.

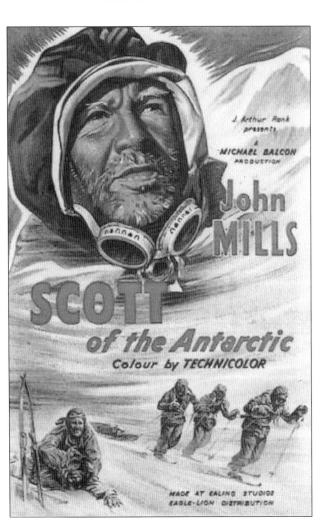

The film was produced by Michael Balcon who was knighted the same year, 1948. He was born in Birmingham in 1896.

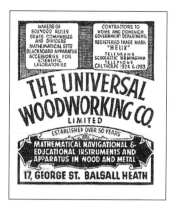

Actor, Noel Johnson, returns to his home city of Birmingham, 1948.
He was born here in 1916 and went on to play the lead in the immensely
popular radio series, "Dick Barton, Special Agent", which first aired on
7th October 1946.

College Road/Couchman Road, Saltley, c 1948.

American food packages, 1948.

Care packages arrive in the city, November 1948. Americans, realising that many British families were living on the breadline, sent parcels of food and clothing.

The Alexandra Theatre auditorium seen from the stage, 1948.

Norman Wisdom appears in "Robinson Crusoe", Alexandra Theatre, Christmas 1948.

Father Christmas arrives at Lewis's, Bull Street, 1948.

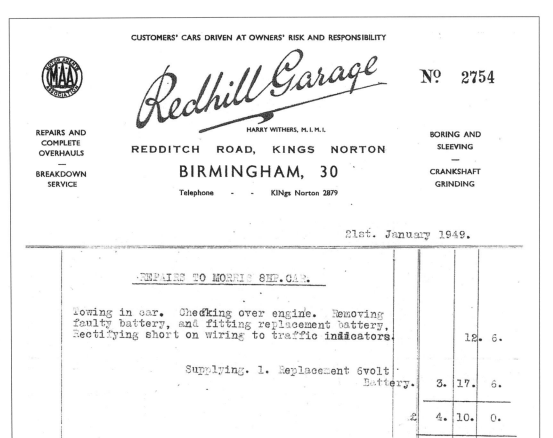

CUSTOMERS' CARS DRIVEN AT OWNERS' RISK AND RESPONSIBILITY

Redhill Garage

HARRY WITHERS, M.I.M.I.

No. 2754

REPAIRS AND
COMPLETE
OVERHAULS
—
BREAKDOWN
SERVICE

REDDITCH ROAD, KINGS NORTON
BIRMINGHAM, 30
Telephone - - KINgs Norton 2879

BORING AND
SLEEVING
—
CRANKSHAFT
GRINDING

21st. January 1949.

REPAIRS TO MORRIS 8HP. CAR.

Towing in car. Checking over engine. Removing
faulty battery, and fitting replacement battery,
Rectifying short on wiring to traffic indicators. 12. 6.

Supplying. 1. Replacement 6volt
Battery. 3. 17. 6.

£ 4. 10. 0.

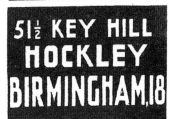

Hill Street, seen from New Street Station (with Navigation Street on the right),
1949.

Kay back at Brum

His many friends in the profession will be delighted to know that, after a seven months' illness, bassist Sid Kay is back with sax-leader Mannie Berg at the Grand Casino, Birmingham.

Sid, pianist Frank Mortimer and Mannie Berg have been together for the past 16 years—which must be a record.

In February, next year, Mannie Berg will have completed four years at this hall. His present line-up is completed by Tommy Allan (drs.) and Sid Bakewell (acc.).

ONCE again Birmingham's Hedley Ward (*inset*) hits the headlines with the news that the Hedley Ward Trio is again to be heard in the Light Programme, when it plays in "Let's Make Music" on February 17 and 24.

On February 11 the full Hedley Ward Band will be heard in the Midland Home Service in "Take Your Partners" (1.40 to 2 p.m.), on March 7 has a "Music While You Work" spot from 3.30 to 4 p.m., and again on March 9 plays a twenty-minute late-night spot in the Midland programme at 10 p.m.

On the following evening (March 10), Hedley and his merry men will play for the Birmingham Pantomime Ball for the second year in succession, and, on the 11th, for the annual Scottish Ball—their third successive appearance.

Anthony E. Pratt, a Birmingham musician and solicitor's clerk, invented the game of "Cluedo" in 1944. It was originally intended as a game that would be played in bomb shelters but, because of wartime shortages, it was not officially launched until 1949.

Dame Hilda Rose, born in Birmingham in 1892, becomes the first female professor of Birmingham University's Medical School in 1949. Her father was a Master Grocer in Balsall Heath.

Made at Chad Valley, Harborne, c 1949.

89

New Inn Road/Birchfield Road, Birchfield, 1949.

Martineau Street, 1949.

A tilting test at Metropolitan Cammel Carriage & Wagon Co. Ltd,
Saltley, 15th March 1949.

An inspector testing a fruiterer's weights, Wholesale Markets, 1949.

How the rubbish was dealt with at the refuse screen and sorting belt, Montague Street Works, Bordesley, 1949.

Princess Elizabeth visits Selly Oak Hospital, 10th May 1949.

Danny Kaye, one of the most accomplished comedy artistes of the age, appears at the Hippodrome, June 1949.

Note the spelling of "Kingston"!

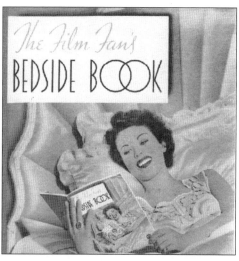

33-SEATER LUXURY COACH BODY BY GORDONS COACHCRAFT LIMITED
199, GOLDEN HILLOCK ROAD, BIRMINGHAM, 11. VIC. 2959

The BBC radio series began in 1948 and won the National Radio Award in 1949. It featured Dick Bentley, Joy Nichols and Jimmy Edwards.

Bournville Darby and Joan Club, c 1949.

Great Lister Street/Windsor Street, Vauxhall, c 1949.

The Wheatsheaf, Latimer Street/Irving Street,
Lee Bank, c 1949.

Corporation Street, 1949.

93

Hill Street, looking towards Navigation Street, November, 1949.

Grand Union Canal, Small Heath, 1949. In the distance can be seen the back of houses in Oldknow Road.

The very first edition, 1949.

95

ACKNOWLEDGEMENTS

(for providing photographs, encouragement and numerous other favours)

Keith Ackrill, The Birmingham City Council Dept of Planning and Architecture; The Birmingham Post and Mail Ltd.; The Late Gordon Bunce; The Late Arthur Camwell; Roy Dillon; John Ellis; Malcolm and Judy Edwards; Simon Fredericks; Raymond Horton; Alfred Jones; Laughton and Sons Ltd.; Pete Lindup; Brian Matthews; Dennis Moore; Garry Owen; David and Jeanette Parkes; Joan Pearks; Keith Price; Maurice Price; Arthur Roe; The Late Derek Salberg; Keith Shakespeare; Roger Smith; Nicky Stevens; Keith Vaughan; Joan Wanty; West Midlands Police; Robert Wilkes; Rosemary Wilkes; Dennis Williams; Keith Williams; Ken Windsor.

Please forgive any possible omissions. Every effort has been made to include all organisations and individuals involved in the book.

The Carlton Dance Orchestra, TA Centre, Barrows Lane, Sheldon 1946. They were the resident band there for 10 years.